Famous Composers in History for Kids! From Beethoven to Bach Music History Edition

Children's Arts, Music & Photography Books

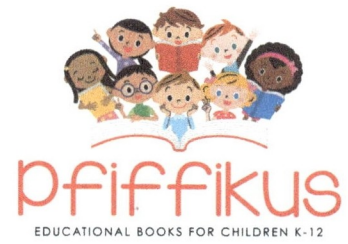

Copyright 2016

All Rights reserved. No part of this book may be reproduced or used in any way or form or by any means whether electronic or mechanical, this means that you cannot record or photocopy any material ideas or tips that are provided in this book

Do you ever wonder who composed your favorite musical compositions? Read on and meet some of them!

Johann Sebastian Bach was a German composer whose work includes the St. Matthew Passion and St John Passion.

Wolfgang Amadeus Mozart was an Austrian composer of the classical era. Mozart composed more than 600 works in different fields, including the Serenade No. 13.

Ludwig van Beethoven was a German composer. He created musical compositions for the symphony orchestra.

Richard Wagner was a German composer known for his opera compositions like Die Laune des Verliebten.

Johannes Brahms was a German composer who was also a pianist. His first composition was Der Abend in 1874.

Franz Schubert was an Austrian composer with over 1,500 works which includes Ave Maria.

Felix Mendelssohn-Bartholdy was a German composer in the Romantic period. His works include Overture to a Midsummer Night's Dream and The Marriage of the Camacho.

Franz Liszt was a Hungarian composer who was once considered the greatest pianist in his period. His works include La Campanella and Hungarian Rhapsody No. 2.

Giuseppe Verdi was an Italian composer who is said to be the most important composer of the Risorgimento (Italian unification).

Giacomo Puccini was an Italian composer whose works are recognized as the most important operas. Edgar and Le Villi are two of his greatest works.

Anton Bruckner was an Austrian composer recognized for his symphony and mass works including Am Grabe and Festlied.

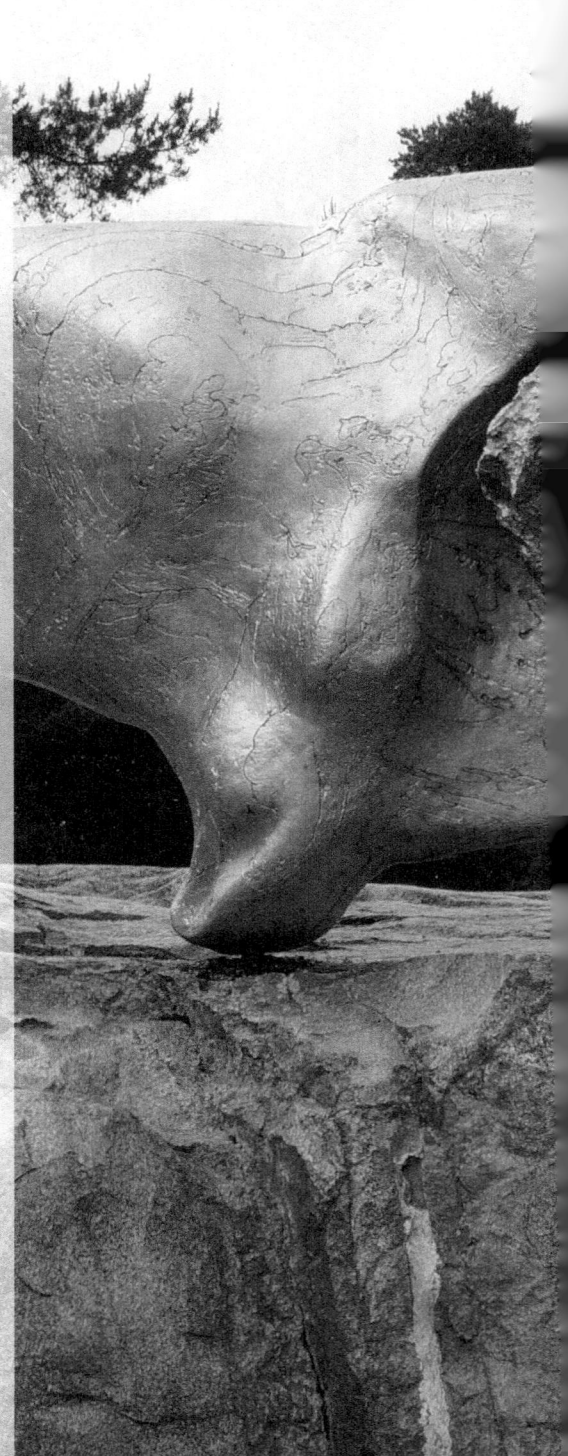

Jean Sibelius was a Finnish composer whose music has helped Finland in its search of independence from Russia. His works include En Saga and Barden.

Edvard Grieg was a Norwegian composer known to have used Norwegian folk music in his works. His compositions include Piano Concerto in A minor and Cello Concerto.

Christoph Willibald Gluck was a German composer whose work includes Orfeo ed Euridice and Alceste.

Christoph Wilibald Ritter von Gluck.

Georges Bizet was a French composer whose work includes Carmen.

Modest Mussorgsky was a Russian composer and is a member of a group called "The Five". His pieces include Boris Godunov and A Night on Bald Mountain.

Johann Strauss Jr. is an Austrian composer known for Viennese waltz and Viennese operettas like Die Fledermaus in 1874.

There are many other great composers. Research and have fun!

Lightning Source UK Ltd.
Milton Keynes UK
UKOW07f1216231017
311498UK00007B/93/P